Extravagant Peace:

100 Simplistic Thoughts to Discover, Embrace, and Cultivate Inner Peace.

Kandra Albury

Extravagant Peace:

100 Simplistic Thoughts to Discover, Embrace, and Cultivate Inner Peace

ISBN (979-8-9874925-8-1)

A special note from the
extravagant peacekeeper:

*May this peace work
encourage you to be an
extravagant steward of
peace. Discover it, embrace
it, cultivate it, and bask in
it. Blessed are the
peacemakers (that's us).
Now, be at peace.*

Prioritize
Evaluate
Arrange
Conscious
Experiences

1

Peace keeps us
grounded.

2

There's pride, then there's peace. They can't co-exist.
~Humility

3

It's impossible to
maintain peace
when you're
attached to chaos.

4

Peace says no.

5

Peace says yes.

6

Peace retreats.

7

If taking your
marbles and going
home means you
have peace, then
start collecting
them.

8

Peace is never
forced or toxic.

9

Find *your* peace, and
your purpose will
reveal itself.

10

Be mindful of how you handle *your* peace; it's a prized possession.

11

When we forfeit our
peace, expect the
opposite—war.

12

Never seek to get
even. ~Peace

13

Peace comes from God, but it's often compromised by man.

14

Peace is doing
what's best for you.
Choose inner peace,
always.

15

Sometimes peace requires us to let go and sometimes it requires us to hold on. You decide.

16

Toxic behavior
uproots peace.

17

Leave a legacy of peace.

18

Seek peace, even
when you don't
sense it.

19

Pray for peace,
daily.

20

May peace to be *your* portion.

21

Minding *your* business produces peace. It's called peace of mind.

22

Beware of
distractions. ~Peace

23

If you've had to
fight to keep *your*
peace, then it
shouldn't be so
easily compromised.

24

Compromising *your* peace also compromises *your* power.

25

Peace requires
setting and
maintaining healthy
boundaries.

26

It wasn't a loss, it
was a lesson.
~Peace.

27

Peace doesn't require having the last say. Let them have it.

28

Allow peace to be
your final answer.

29

Peace has its place…it belongs in *your* heart.

30

Peace has a tone.

31

Kindness is a bridge
to peace.

32

Acquiring peace takes time. It is a repetitive practice.

33

Don't be a peace
breaker.

34

A peacemaker has a
happy heart.

35

Forgiveness doesn't mean you lost; it means you're free.

36

Peace is absolutely
possible. However,
it must be a daily
habit.

37

Pray for peace and
call a therapist if
you must.

38

If you don't have
peace… ask
yourself, why?

39

Peace is a prized
state of being, so
cherish it.

40

Being at peace *with* yourself is a privilege.

41

You don't owe anyone an explanation regarding the preservation of *your* inner peace.

42

If explaining *your* peace causes anxiety, save your words.

43

Let there be peace
on Earth, within
you and everyone
connected to you.

44

Control *your* thoughts and actions, they're connected to *your* inner peace.

45

As you prioritize
your life, may peace
be *your* portion.

46

When we
compromise our
peace, we
compromise so
much more!

47

A world full of
peace, is a world we
can all love.

48

When peace is our
priority, kindness
and love are
inevitable.

49

Peace reduces stress, prioritize *your* peace.

50

Say this aloud, I live
for peace.

51

May your eyes be
the windows to *your*
inner peace.

52

If you're not a
peacemaker, you're
a troublemaker.

53

Promise yourself to
be a keeper of
peace.

54

Encouraging words
uplift and bring
peace.

55

Peace is deciding if, what and when to share. Some things are sacred.

56

Peace should be one
of *your* main
personal attributes.

57

A soft no or even a
stern no *will*
guarantee peace.

58

Your first choice and
final option *should*
be peace.

59

Work to be at peace
with yourself, it's a
necessity. ~Peace

60

Peace is being
integral with *your*
words, *your* tone,
and *your* actions.

61

Peace is *never* nasty.

62

Peace relents with
gratitude.

63

Peace has its perks;
peace of mind is
one of them.

64

Peace understands that people will enter our lives, so welcome them. However, they will also leave us, so release them. Then some will stay; so, value them.

65

Learn the lesson,
accept it peace*fully*
but leave the pain
behind.

66

Peace is knowing
when enough is
enough.

67

...Oh, what peace
we often forfeit, oh
what needless pains
we bear, all because
we choose to carry
everything *ourselve*s
and forfeit prayer.

68

Incessant people pleasing leads to comprised peace.

69

Allow *your* takeaway
to always be peace.

70

Come in peace, go in peace. Whenever possible choose peace.

Whenever possible, follow peace with all men, for without no man shall see God.
[Hebrews 12:14]

72

Pray for inner peace
and world peace,
daily, and we will
have them.

73

No need to prove
yourself. ~Peace

If it doesn't kill you,
it could be robbing
you of *your* peace.
Change that, *now!*

75

The opposite of peace is chaos. The opposite of chaos is peace. Choose the latter.

76

Your words matter.
So, use them wisely.
~Peace

77

Whenever possible
encourage peace.

78

Humility produces
peace and vice
versa.

79

When you speak
allow others to hear
your inner peace and
not *your* ego.

80

Peace is a restorer
of grace and dignity.

81

The tone of peace is compassion; we *can* sense it.

82

No matter what,
keep your peace
intact.

83

Where there is no peace, contentment doesn't exist.

84

When you think,
think peace.

85

Allow peace to be *your* portion and *your* guide.

86

Choose peace and
not fear.

87

Healthy boundaries
protect *your* peace.

88

You *may* have to
secure your borders
to protect your
peace. Do it!
~Peace

89

Do not isolate
yourself for too
long. Be sure to
maintain balance.
~Peace

90

Peace is a state of
mind, heart, and
spirit.

91

There's peace in
knowing you have
peace.

92

When others think
they've won, allow
them to think just
that. ~Peace

93

We reap what we sow. Nothing compares to a harvest of peace.

94

Your peace is non-
negotiable.

95

Mind how you
spend *your* time and
who you spend it
with. ~Peace

96

Have faith as you trust God in the process. ~Peace

97

You cannot pretend
to have peace; either
you have it, or you
don't.

98

Peace agents are
change agents.

99

Bet on peace and
you will always win!

100

Just be done with it.
~Peace

BONUS

Choose peace...
whatever that
looks like.

Kandra Charalene Albury is an extravagant peacekeeper, servant leader, author, children's advocate, and business strategist. She is also the Co-CEO and Founder of More Than Expected (MTE) Publishing, a full-service publishing and branding agency based in Gainesville, FL.

She earned a bachelor's degree in communication from the University of North Florida and a master's degree in mass communication from the University of Florida. She has a Ph.D. in ministerial education from Truth Bible University, and she is a proud product of the Putnam County School System. She has more than 15 years of executive-level and [C-suite] communication experience.

Kandra is married to James C. Albury. They are honored to be the parents of three amazing children and an awesome grandson.

She is a member of Zeta Phi Beta Sorority, Inc. Gainesville's Delta Sigma Zeta Chapter.

When Kandra isn't serving in the Kingdom or coaching her clients, she is enjoying warm sunsets at nearby Florida beaches.

ExtravagantPeace.com